THE MICROWAVE
Shakespeare

Other titles in the series

*Hamlet
Julius Caesar
Macbeth
The Merchant of Venice
A Midsummer Night's Dream
Romeo and Juliet
The Tempest
Twelfth Night*

MUCH ADO ABOUT NOTHING

Barbara Catchpole
&
Stephen Rickard

Illustrated by Margit van der Zwan

Much Ado About Nothing
Published by Ransom Publishing Ltd.
Unit 7, Brocklands Farm, West Meon, Hampshire GU32 1JN, UK
www.ransom.co.uk

ISBN   978 178591 635 9
First published in 2019

Copyright © 2019 Ransom Publishing Ltd.
Text copyright © 2019 Ransom Publishing Ltd.
Cover illustration copyright ©SvitDen
Illustrations copyright © Margit van der Zwan; Flannymagic; chrupka. Globe theatre today: claudiodivizia. Original Globe theatre illustration: C. Walter Hodges, licensed under the Creative Commons Attribution-Share Alike 4.0 International (https://creativecommons.org/licenses/by-sa/4.0/deed.en) license.

A CIP catalogue record of this book is available from the British Library.

All rights reserved. No part of this publication may be reproduced, stored in a retrieval system, or transmitted, in any form or by any means, electronic, mechanical, photocopying, recording or otherwise, without the prior permission of the publishers.

The rights of Barbara Catchpole and Stephen Rickard to be identified as the authors and of Margit van der Zwan to be identified as the illustrator of this Work have been asserted by them in accordance with sections 77 and 78 of the Copyright, Design and Patents Act 1988.

CONTENTS

Where	6
When	7
Who	8
The Globe Theatre	11
One	12
Two	22
Three	34
Four	38
What's the play about?	54
What are the main themes in the play?	56
Shakespeare's words	59

WHERE

The play is set in **Messina**, a port on the island of **Sicily**, which is just next to the 'foot' of Italy.

WHEN

We don't know when the events in the play take place, but the play is probably set in Shakespeare's time (that is, his 'present').

The play itself was probably written in 1598 and 1599.

WHO

Don Pedro – Prince of Arragon

Leonato – Governor of Messina

Claudio – a young Lord of Florence

Don Pedro   Leonato   Claudio

Beatrice – Leonato's niece

Antonio – Leonato's brother

Hero – Leonato's daughter

Benedick – a young Lord of Padua

Don John – Don Pedro's illegitimate (bastard) brother

Beatrice   Benedick   Don John

Balthazar – servant to Don Pedro

Borachio – follower of Don John
Conrade – follower of Don John

Margaret)
Ursula) – Hero's ladies-in-waiting

Dogberry – a constable
Verges – Dogberry's assistant

Friar Francis

A sexton

HELPFUL NOTE

All the spoken words in this book that are in italics, *'like this'*, are actual words taken from Shakespeare's play. They are spoken by one of the actors in the play.

The Globe Theatre. Above is a reconstruction of the original Globe Theatre, which is in London. Below is a cross-section of the original theatre, which was built in 1599.

Shakespeare's plays were performed at this theatre. When you read this book, just imagine standing in the crowd, in front of this stage, watching the play.

ONE

At his house in Messina, **Leonato**, the Governor of Messina, is with his daughter **Hero** and his niece **Beatrice**. A messenger arrives to tell them that **Don Pedro**, Prince of Arragon, is arriving in Messina today.

Don Pedro has been in battle, but thankfully not many people were hurt. The messenger tells them that Don Pedro has honoured a young man from Florence named **Claudio**, who was very brave in battle.

'He looks like a lamb but fights like a lion,' the messenger tells Leonato.

'Has **Benedick of Padua** returned from battle?' Beatrice asks.

'*O, he's returned; and as pleasant as ever he was,*' the messenger replies. 'He provided good service in these wars.'

'You mean you had rotten food and he helped you eat it,' replies Beatrice sharply.

Leonato explains to the messenger that '*There is a kind of merry war* between Beatrice and Signior Benedick. Every time they meet *there's a skirmish of wit between them.*'

'And I always win,' adds Beatrice. 'Last time we fought, he got so confused that at the end he was about as smart as his horse.'

'I see you don't like this man,' observes the messenger dryly.

'No,' replies Beatrice. 'And who's his new friend? He always has a new friend.'

'He spends a lot of time with Claudio.'

'*O Lord,*' replies Beatrice, '*he will hang upon him like a disease!* Benedick is easier to catch than the plague. *God help the noble Claudio!*'

'I'm going to make sure I stay on the right side of you, lady,' the messenger tells her.

'Do that.'

Then (thankfully) Don Pedro arrives, followed by Claudio, Benedick himself, Don Pedro's servant **Balthazar**, and **Don John**, Don Pedro's illegitimate brother.

Don Pedro turns to Hero. 'Is this your daughter?' he asks Leonato.

Leonato chuckles. 'That's what her mother always tells me!'

'Did you doubt she was your daughter?' Benedick asks Leonato.

'No, because then you were only a child, Benedick. So you couldn't have seduced my wife.'

'He's got you there!' Don Pedro laughs.

Don Pedro and Leonato move aside to talk business, so Beatrice turns to Benedick. 'Why are you still talking, Signior Benedick? Nobody's listening to you!'

'Oh, *Lady Disdain*. Are you still alive?' he replies. And they're off again, hurling insults at each other.

'All ladies love me, except you,' says Benedick. 'But actually, I don't love anyone.'

'Lucky for women!' Beatrice is straight back at him. 'And I'm the same. I don't love anyone. *I had rather hear my dog bark at a crow than a man swear he loves me.*' And on it goes.

Then Don Pedro and Leonato are back. Leonato has invited them all to stay with him for at least a month.

'You too, Don John. Now you and your brother [Don Pedro] are friends again, you are welcome.'

They all go inside Leonato's house, except for Claudio and Benedick, who stay outside.

'Did you see Leonato's daughter?' Claudio asks Benedick.

'I saw her, but I didn't notice her.'

'What do you think of her?' Claudio presses.

'To be honest? She's too low for high praise, too dark for fair praise and too little for great praise. If she looked any different, she'd be ugly.' Benedick thinks he's made rather a good joke, but Claudio is serious.

'Why, are you thinking of buying her?' asks Benedick.

'You can't buy a jewel such as Hero,' Claudio answers. *'In mine eye she is the sweetest lady that ever I looked on.'*

OK, he's smitten.

'I don't see it really,' says Benedick. 'Now Beatrice, she's much more beautiful. But she has such a temper … Anyway, you're not thinking of marrying Hero, are you?'

'If she says, "Yes"!'

'Oh for Heaven's sake!' Benedict explodes.

'Isn't there one man left in the world who knows that you should not get married!'

Then Don Pedro strolls past on his way to the garden. 'What are you two talking about?' he asks. 'Tell me, Benedick! Your loyalty to me means you have to tell me.'

'Well, if it's an order: Claudio here is in love with Hero!'

'She is a worthy lady,' Don Pedro says.

'That I love her, I feel,' Claudio blurts out.

'I don't feel or know anything!' Benedict laughs. 'Burn me at the stake and I'll not change my mind!'

'You never did believe in the power of beauty … ' Don Pedro tells him.

'… or in the power of reason,' Claudio adds.

'Listen,' says Benedick. 'A woman conceived me. I give thanks for that! She brought me up – *humble thanks* again. But I don't trust women and I will live my life as a single man!'

'Benedick, I swear,' says Don Pedro, *'I shall see thee, ere I die, look pale with love.'*

'With anger, with sickness or with hunger, my lord, not with love. If I'm ever pale with love, jab out my eyes with a love poet's pen. You can *hang me in a bottle like a cat and shoot at me.*'

And with that, Benedick leaves them.

So now Don Pedro and Claudio are alone. Time for a serious chat. Claudio asks Don Pedro for some help.

'Before I went to battle, I looked at Hero *with a soldier's eye,*' Claudio tells him. 'I liked her, but had more important things to worry about. But now I'm back, my thoughts of war have all gone and into their place *Come thronging soft and delicate desires,*

All prompting me how fair young Hero is.'

Don Pedro is full of encouragement. '*If thou dost love fair Hero, cherish it,*

And I will break with her and with her father,
And thou shalt have her.'

There's a masked party tonight, Don Pedro tells Claudio. Don Pedro says he will disguise himself as Claudio for the party and will pour out 'his' feelings to Hero. Then he'll talk to her father. 'And then, Claudio, she'll be yours.'

What could possibly go wrong?

In Leonato's house, Leonato is fussing about the music for the evening party. **Antonio**, his brother, has some news.

'Listen, Leonato. My servant overheard Don Pedro and Claudio talking earlier. Don Pedro told Claudio that he loves Hero. He's going to ask her at the party tonight, and if she says "Yes", he's going to tell you about it at once.'

'*Hath the fellow any wit that told you this?*' Leonato asks.

'He's a *good sharp fellow*. Talk to him yourself!'

'No, it's fine,' replies Leonato. 'But Hero should know about this in advance. Will you go and tell her for me?'

Oops!

Elsewhere in the house, Don John is with his friend **Conrade**. Don John is feeling very gloomy.

'You should listen to reason,' Conrade tells him.

'And when I've listened, what blessings does it bring?' Don John replies. '*I cannot hide what I am.* I will be sad when I have reason to be sad, just as I'll eat when I'm hungry and sleep when I'm tired.'

'Yes,' says Conrade, 'but you need to watch it. Not long ago you opposed your brother, and he's only just forgiven you.

You need to be careful if you're going to stay in his favour.'

'Huh. I'd rather be a weed in a hedge than a rose in Don Pedro's garden. I prefer to be looked down on by everybody than to put on a show of being nice and tricking people into liking me. You can't say I'm an honest man, but at least you can say I'm a *plain-dealing villain.*'

Then another friend of Don John, **Borachio** comes in, all excited. 'I have news of a marriage! Claudio is to marry Hero! Don Pedro is going to get her to say "Yes" and then he will give her to Claudio. I was spying on them. I heard it all.'

'Pretty boy Claudio,' mutters Don John. 'Come on, let's go to the dance. Claudio was the one who stopped me getting power over my brother. If I can make things difficult for him in any way, it'll make me very happy. Will you two help me?'

'*To the death, my lord,*' says Conrade.

TWO

Leonato, Antonio, Hero and Beatrice are at Leonato's. The party is starting soon.

'How sour Don John always looks!' Beatrice laughs. 'Whenever I see him, I get heartburn!'

'*He is of a very melancholy disposition,*' Hero says sweetly.

'What we need,' says Beatrice, 'is a man half-way between Benedick and Don John. One of them is like a painting – he never speaks – and the other chatters mindlessly like a little boy. But that man, *with money enough in his purse, such a man would win any woman in the world, if a' could get her good-will.'*

'Really, niece,' laughs Leonato, 'you'll never get a husband with a tongue like yours!'

'I hope not! I won't take a husband until God makes men out of something other than dirt.'

Leonato speaks gently to Hero. 'Remember, if Prince Don Pedro asks you to marry him, you know your answer!'

The partygoers begin to arrive. Don Pedro, Claudio, Benedick, Balthazar and Don John all come in, wearing masks. The party begins.

Don Pedro asks Hero to dance with him. They flirt gently. 'I hope your face isn't as ugly as your mask,' says Hero.

Hero's gentlewomen (or ladies-in-waiting) **Margaret** and **Ursula** dance too; Margaret dances with Balthazar and Ursula and Antonio dance together.

Then Beatrice and Benedick dance together – but because they're both masked, neither knows who their partner is.

'Tell me who you are!' Beatrice asks.

'Not now.'

'You say someone said I was stuck-up and got my conversation from a joke book? It must be Benedick who said that!'

'Who's he?' asks Benedick.

'Why he is a *very dull fool*. Nobody with any sense likes him and he tells impossible lies.'

'I'll tell him you said that.'

'Go ahead!' Beatrice flutters her fan. 'Tell him! He'll say a few nasty things about me, too.'

Everybody is dancing – except Don John, his friend **Borachio** and one other masked man.

'Who's that guy over there?' asks Don John.

'It's Claudio,' replies Borachio. '*I know him by his bearing.*'

Don John walks up to Claudio. 'Are you Signior Benedick?' (What's he playing at?)

'I am,' replies Claudio.

'Sir, my brother is in love with Hero. Please make him change his mind – she's too common to marry a prince.'

'I heard him swear he loves her – and he's going to marry her tonight,' adds Borachio.

Don John and Borachio leave. Now that he's alone, Claudio removes his mask.

'I said I was Benedick, but I hear this *ill news* with Claudio's ears,' Claudio says to himself. 'So the prince wants Hero for himself. Friendships do last forever, but not where love is involved. *Let every eye negotiate for itself*

And trust no agent; for beauty is a witch whose charms can turn loyalty into passion. Therefore goodbye, Hero.'

So Don John has a cunning plan to turn Claudio against Hero – and it's working!

Then Benedick enters. 'Claudio. The prince has got your Hero.'

'I wish him joy of her,' Claudio replies sharply. 'Now please leave me alone.'

With that, he walks out. Has Claudio really given up on Hero?

Don Pedro strolls over to Benedick. 'Did you see Claudio?'

'I did, and he's not happy,' replies Benedick. 'I told him you've won this lady's heart – that's true, isn't it? You've stolen his bird's nest?'

'No, of course not. I'm just teaching the little birds to sing. Then I'll return them to their rightful owner.'

'We'll see!' Benedick isn't convinced.

Don Pedro changes the subject. 'Benedick, Lady Beatrice is upset with you. The man she danced with said you insulted her.'

'Huh! She insulted me! She told me – not realising it was me – that I was *the prince's jester*, that I was duller than mud. She speaks daggers, *and every word stabs*. If her breath were as terrible as her words, she'd kill everything from here to the north star.

While she's around it's quieter in hell and people sin on purpose, just to be sent to hell to avoid her. I will not marry her.'

'Here she comes!' Don Pedro laughs, as Beatrice, Hero, Leonato and Claudio enter.

Benedick turns to Don Pedro. 'Your grace, please send me on an urgent mission *to the world's end*. I'll do anything to avoid exchanging three words with this *harpy*.' Then he runs off.

Beatrice has brought Claudio with her.

'Claudio, what's wrong?' Don Pedro teases.

'Nothing,' he replies sulkily.

'Claudio, cheer up!' Don Pedro says. '*I have wooed in thy name, and fair Hero is won: I have broke with her father, and his good will obtained.* You just need to name the day of marriage.'

Leonato hugs Claudio. 'Count, my daughter is yours – *and with her my fortunes.*'

Suddenly Claudio is beside himself with happiness. '*Lady, as you are mine, I am yours.*'

'Say something, Hero,' Beatrice laughs, 'or, if you can't, *stop his mouth with a kiss.*'

Don Pedro smiles. 'Beatrice, *you have a merry heart.* Now I will find you a husband!' He pauses. 'Will you have me, my lady?'

'No, your grace. You are too expensive to wear every day. I'd need another husband for weekdays.'

She rushes off.

'She is always happy,' Don Pedro says, 'but she can't bear to think of having a husband ... Although she would make an excellent wife for Benedick!'

Claudio wants to get married at once, but Leonato says he needs a week to prepare. Then Don Pedro has a brilliant idea.

'OK, I'm going to use the week before you get married *to bring Signior Benedick and the Lady Beatrice into a mountain of affection* with each other. I'm sure we can make a match! Benedick isn't the worst husband and I'm sure we can make them fall for each other.'

The others all agree to help. It's time to get to work!

Don John is talking with Borachio. 'So Claudio will marry Leonato's daughter,' he says.

'Yes, but I can stop it,' replies Borachio.

'Any obstacle to Claudio's happiness is like medicine to me. I hate him,' says Don John bitterly. 'How will you do it, Borachio?'

'Go and tell your brother he made a terrible mistake matching Claudio and Hero. Tell them Hero really loves me. Then bring them to Hero's window the night before the wedding. Hero's lady-in-waiting, Margaret, likes me – I'll make sure they see Margaret and myself at the window. I'll call her "Hero" and they'll think it's her. The wedding will be called off instantly.'

'I like it! Let's do it,' says Don John.

Benedick is amazed at the change in Claudio. 'He used to laugh at how love made men soppy, but now here he is doing exactly that. Claudio was a man who would walk ten miles to see a good suit of armour; now he's lying awake for ten nights thinking how he should dress for the wedding.'

Could love change Benedick like that? *I cannot tell; I think not.* But I can say this: until I really fall in love, no woman will make a fool of me.'

Benedick sees Don Pedro, Leonato, and Claudio turning up, so he quickly hides behind a big hedge. The trouble is, Don Pedro and Claudio can see him; they know he's there!

'Let's have some fun,' Claudio whispers to Don Pedro.

'Come here, Leonato,' says Don Pedro. 'What was it you were telling me? That your niece, Beatrice, is in love with Signior Benedick?'

'I thought she hated him!' says Leonato. 'But it's true, she absolutely adores him! *She loves him with an enraged affection.*'

Benedick can't believe what he's hearing. 'What symptoms of love has she got? And has she told Benedick?' Don Pedro asks Leonato.

'*Bait the hook well; this fish will bite,*' Claudio mutters in Leonato's ear.

'No, she hasn't told Benedick – *and swears she never will,*' replies Leonato. 'That's the thing that's driving her crazy.'

Now Claudio lays it on thick. 'She falls down to her knees, weeps, beats her chest and tears her hair, crying "*O sweet Benedick. God give me patience!*" '

'We should tell Benedick.' Don Pedro says.

'No. He would just torment her even more,' says Claudio. 'Now, come on, let's go. Dinner is ready.'

They leave Benedick on his own, still behind the hedge. He is amazed. He has always thought that Beatrice is intelligent and beautiful. 'If she loves me, well that love must be returned! I said I'd never marry, but ... '

Suddenly Beatrice appears before him. 'Sir, against my will, I've been sent to tell you dinner is ready.'

'Beautiful Beatrice, thank you for your trouble.'

'No trouble. If it was any trouble I wouldn't have done it.'

'Yep, she's definitely in love with me!' Benedick thinks.

THREE

In Leonato's garden, Hero is working on the plan to get Benedick and Beatrice hooked up.

'Margaret, go into the house and find Beatrice. Tell her you overheard Ursula and I talking about her. Get her to come and spy on what we are saying!'

So, as Beatrice secretly listens in, Hero tells Ursula that Benedick secretly loves Beatrice. 'He wants to tell her, but she is so proud and tough. *Disdain and scorn ride sparkling in her eyes.* She loves herself so much, she can't love anybody else. Who would dare tell her?'

'But you must tell her!'

'No. I'm going to persuade Benedick *to fight against his passion.*'

'But surely she's not going to refuse *so rare a gentleman* as Benedick?' Ursula asks.

'He's the only worthy man in Italy – apart from my Claudio, of course,' adds Hero.

They leave to look at wedding clothes.

Beatrice cannot believe what she has heard! 'Can this be true? Do people criticise me so much for my scorn and pride? Then I will stop such behaviour. Benedick, keep on loving me and I will return that love, and we will seal it with a wedding ring.'

It's the day before Claudio and Hero's wedding. Don John finds Don Pedro and Claudio together. Putting Borachio's plan into effect, Don John tells them both that Hero is being unfaithful. She is being worse than wicked. He promises to show them tonight at her bedroom window.

Claudio is upset, but he is also angry. 'If I see anything tonight that gives me a reason not to marry her tomorrow, then I will shame her,' he tells them both.

That night, Constable **Dogberry** is deploying his watchmen. He tells them to stop all men they meet, but to keep quiet and stay out of the way. 'And keep watch over Leonato's house, because there's a wedding there tomorrow … '

Two of the watchmen then happen to overhear Borachio and Conrade talking. Borachio tells Conrade how he's been given a thousand ducats by Don John to set up Don Pedro and Claudio into thinking they see Hero being unfaithful. They thought they were watching her kiss another man, he says, but in fact the two people they saw were Borachio himself and Margaret.

The watchmen don't really understand what was being said, but they decide they've heard enough to be suspicious. So they arrest Conrade and Borachio!

In Hero's apartment, Margaret is helping Hero into her wedding dress. Margaret is chattering away. (Does she feel guilty?)

Hero says, 'My heart feels heavy.'

'You will soon be heavier with a man on top of you!' says Margaret. Hero is embarrassed by Margaret's joke; she is so innocent.

'Now help me get dressed,' says Hero.

In Leonato's house, Dogberry and his assistant **Verges** are reporting to Leonato. They caught two suspicious men last night and they think Leonato should see them.

But no, Leonato has a wedding to go to; he's too busy. 'Just do it yourself and report back!' he tells them.

(Bad decision, Leonato.)

FOUR

At the church, Claudio and Hero stand in front of the priest. It is their wedding ceremony. Don Pedro, Don John, Leonato, Benedick and Beatrice stand behind them.

'Will you give me your daughter?' Claudio asks Leonato.

'Freely my son,' says Leonato.

'Well, you can have her back!' shouts Claudio. 'Take her back, Leonato. *Give not this rotten orange to your friend.*'

OK. Looks like the wedding's not going to happen!

'She only appears honourable,' says

Claudio. 'Look, she's blushing like a virgin. But her blush is guilt, not modesty. She has slept with another man.'

'Are you ill, my lord?' Hero asks Claudio. 'Is that why you're saying this?'

'Hero, you are no maiden,' says Don Pedro. 'Leonato, on my honour, last night we saw her with *a ruffian* who has now confessed that he's been with you a thousand times.'

Poor Hero is confused. 'What? It wasn't me!' she says. Then she faints.

'Come on, let's go.' Don Pedro, Don John and Claudio leave the church.

Beatrice rushes to Hero. 'I think she's dead,' she says, holding Hero's head and fanning her.

'She is better off dead,' says Leonato. 'I was so proud of her and now she has fallen so low.'

'*Oh, on my soul,*' Beatrice cries, 'they are lying about Hero.'

'Do you know for certain?' Benedick asks Beatrice. 'Were you with her last night?'

'No, but I usually sleep in her room.'

'They would not lie!' Leonato is angry and hurt. 'Let her die!'

The priest feels he cannot let this go on any longer. 'I know a lot about people,' he tells them. 'You get to learn a lot in my line of work. And I have been watching Hero's reactions. I think she is innocent and someone has made a huge mistake!'

As Hero wakes from her faint, the priest asks her, 'Hero, what man are they talking about?'

'I don't know! Ask them! Father, honestly,

you can torture me to death if I have been with any man.'

'I think the princes are mistaken,' says the priest.

'If we've been tricked, I blame Don John, *John the bastard*,' says Benedick.

Leonato doesn't know what to think. 'If they are right, I will punish her. But if they have slandered her, then they will have to deal with me.'

'I've got an idea,' says the priest. 'The princes left Hero for dead. Hide her and pretend she really is dead. Prepare for her funeral. That way, when Claudio hears she died from his words, he will feel remorse. And often we don't value what we have until we lose it. If he has lost her, everything might just sort itself out.'

He pauses. 'And if it doesn't work out, you'll just have to put her in a nunnery.'

They all leave – except Benedick and Beatrice. Beatrice has been crying the whole time.

'I think your cousin has been wrongly accused,' Benedick tells her.

'The man who proves that can ask anything of me,' Beatrice replies.

'Beatrice, *I do love nothing in the world so well as you: is not that strange?*'

Finally Beatrice blurts it out. She loves him too. '*I love you with so much of my heart that none is left to protest.*'

'I'll do anything for you,' says Benedick.

'Then kill Claudio.'

'No.'

'Then, if you kill my request, you kill me. Goodbye, Benedick.'

'Wait … '

But Beatrice is furious at Claudio. '*O God, that I were a man! I would eat his heart in the market-place.*'

Benedick wants to help her. 'You're sure that your cousin has been wronged? Then I'll challenge Claudio to a duel. I'll make him pay dearly for this.'

At the prison where Conrade and Borachio are being held, Dogberry is questioning his prisoners. Slowly the whole story of how they have set up Hero comes out.

The **sexton** is appalled. 'Prince John secretly left Messina first thing this morning. Hero was accused just as you've described, and she suddenly died of grief. We must tell Leonato!'

At Leonato's house, Antonio is trying to tell Leonato to calm down, but he won't have it. Leonato says that in his soul he believes that Hero is innocent.

Then Don Pedro and Claudio come in. Leonato tries to explain to them that they must have been wrong about Hero, but Don Pedro says he's in a bit of a hurry.

That is enough to infuriate Leonato. 'In a hurry? A hurry? Claudio, you have wronged me. *Thou hast so wrong'd mine innocent child* and now *she lies buried with her ancestors.* I challenge you to a duel!'

'Leonato, you've got it wrong,' pleads Don Pedro.

'He'll have to kill both of us,' Antonio butts in. 'Claudio will have to fight me first.'

Don Pedro tries again. '*My heart is sorry for your daughter's death,*

But, on my honor, she was charged with nothing

But what was true and very full of proof.'

Antonio and Leonato storm off just as Benedick enters. Surely he will cheer them up with some jokes.

'Welcome,' says Don Pedro. 'You've just missed what was almost a fight.'

But Benedick is not there to chat. Straight away, he challenges Claudio to a duel. (That's three duels; Claudio's going to be very busy!)

'*You are a villain; I jest not,*' Benedick tells him. 'You have killed a sweet lady and you will pay. Let me know when and where.'

They try to joke with him, but he is serious. '*Your brother the bastard* has run away and you two have killed a sweet and innocent lady – you and I will have it out.' Benedick leaves.

'He's serious,' mutters Don Pedro. 'But didn't he say my brother has run away? Hmm … '

Then Dogberry drags Borachio and Conrade in front of Don Pedro and Claudio.

Dogberry explains their offence in his usual pompous way: 'Well sir, they've lied; moreover, they have said things that were not true; secondarily, they are slanderers; sixth and lastly, they have falsely accused a lady; thirdly, they have confirmed things that did not in fact happen; and, in conclusion, they are lying scoundrels.'

So at last it all comes out; Borachio explains it all. Don John paid them to do it. Margaret was all dressed up in Hero's clothes and Borachio kissed her. Don Pedro and Claudio were deceived and then came the terrible wedding …

Don Pedro is horrified. 'This speech runs like iron through my blood.'

'I feel I have drunk poison,' says Claudio. 'My sweet Hero!'

Leonato and Antonio are brought in by the sexton. Leonato looks at Borachio, Don Pedro and Claudio. He is feeling very bitter. '*I thank you, princes, for my daughter's death:*

Record it with your high and worthy deeds: it was very brave of you.'

'I don't know how to ask for your forgiveness,' Claudio and Don Pedro ask Leonato helplessly. 'What can we do?'

'I can't ask you to bring my daughter back to life. But I do ask you both to tell people around Messina how she is innocent. Visit Hero's tomb and sing a tribute to her tonight. My brother here has a daughter almost the spitting image of Hero. We will still become family. Claudio, you will marry this daughter tomorrow morning. Then I will let my desire for revenge die.'

Claudio is very grateful. It could have been a lot worse! '*O noble sir,*

Your over-kindness doth wring tears from me!'

Benedick has come to tell Beatrice that he has challenged Claudio to a duel. But he wants to talk about the two of them, as well.

'And now, Beatrice, *tell me for which of my bad parts didst thou first fall in love with me?*'

'And *for which of my good parts did you first suffer love for me?*' Straight back at him! They can't leave it alone, these two.

They had been joking about, but suddenly Benedick is serious. 'Beatrice, how are you, really? How is Hero?'

'*Very ill*. And I am *very ill too*,' Beatrice admits.

Ursula comes rushing in. 'You must come, madam. There is a right old row at home! Lady Hero was falsely accused! The prince and Claudio were deceived and Don John, who was behind it all, has run off! Come on!'

'Are you coming with me to hear the news?' Beatrice asks Benedick.

'*I will live in thy heart, die in thy lap, and be buried in thy eyes; and moreover, I will go with thee to thy uncle's.*'

That's a 'Yes', then.

Don Pedro and Claudio are at the Leonato family tomb. Claudio hangs an epitaph on Hero's tomb, proclaiming her innocence.

'Here lies Hero, *Done to death by slanderous tongues.* Now I will say goodnight to your bones, Hero. I will do this rite every year.'

Dawn is coming and now Claudio must go to marry a girl he's never even met.

At Leonato's house, Leonato, Antonio, Benedick, Beatrice and Hero have gathered. Everybody feels a bit happier. Hero is innocent (and still alive!), Claudio and Don Pedro are innocent and nobody has to fight Claudio.

Don Pedro and Claudio will arrive in a moment. Leonato sends all the ladies next door, and tells them not to come back in until he says. And when they do, they should all be wearing masks.

Quickly Benedick asks Leonato's permission

to marry Beatrice. Leonato is happy to give it.

Then Don Pedro and Claudio arrive. Claudio confirms he's still happy to marry Antonio's daughter.

So the ladies all come back in, wearing their masks, and Claudio meets his future wife. But Leonato won't let her take her mask off: 'No, not until Claudio takes her hand and swears to marry her.'

*'Give me your hand: before this holy friar,
I am your husband, if you like of me,'*
swears Claudio.

Then his wife-to-be (it is of course Hero) removes her mask. *'And when I lived, I was your other wife.'*

'Another Hero!' exclaims Claudio.

'Yes. One Hero died slandered. But I live, and as surely as I live, I am a virgin.'

'Hero!' Don Pedro is amazed (and very pleased). *'Hero that is dead!'*

'She was only dead as long as people thought the slander was true,' Leonato tells them.

Wait! There is a priest here ... all his friends are here ... it's a good time ...

... so Benedick decides to seize the moment ...

He asks the masked women, 'Which one of you is Beatrice?'

'Me. What do you want?'

'Do you love me?'

'Why, no; no more than reason.'

'Your uncle, the prince and Claudio swore you loved me,' Benedick replies.

'Do you love me?' Beatrice asks.

'Truly – *no more than reason.*'

'Well my cousin, Margaret, and Ursula swore you did.'

'*They swore that you were almost sick for me,*' Benedick tells her.

'*They swore that you were well-nigh dead for me,*' Beatrice replies.

'OK,' says Benedick. 'So you don't love me.'

(Get on with it!)

'Come on,' says Leonato. 'I am sure you love him.'

'And he loves her!' Claudio says quickly. 'Here's a rotten poem he wrote for her!'

'And here's another poem,' says Hero, 'from Beatrice to Benedick!'

'Come,' Benedick tells Beatrice, 'I will marry you, but only because I feel sorry for you!'

'Well,' says Beatrice 'I won't say "No",

but only to save your life, because I hear you are making yourself ill.'

'*Peace! I will stop your mouth.*' Benedick stops her mouth with a kiss.

So Hero and Claudio will be married, and Benedick and Beatrice will be married too. It is time to celebrate!

Just as they are all to dance, a messenger arrives: Don John has been captured and brought back to Messina.

'Don't think about him until tomorrow,' says Benedick. 'I'll think up some great punishments for him. Now, musicians, play!'

What's the play about?

Nowadays we understand the title of this play to mean, 'A lot of fuss about nothing'.

In Shakespeare's time the word 'noting' was pronounced just like 'nothing', and it meant 'gossip' and 'rumour'. So, to Shakespeare's audience, the title also meant, 'A lot of fuss about gossip and rumour'.

The play is a comedy about two couples: Claudio and Hero, and Benedick and Beatrice. At the end of the play both couples are happy and about to be married, but the story of how this comes to pass involves some practical jokes and quite a lot of deceit. Some of this deceit is just for fun, but some is intended to hurt people.

Much Ado About Nothing is usually seen

as one of Shakespeare's best comedies; it combines some genuinely funny scenes with more serious elements.

The title of the play claims that it is not about very much, but in fact the play does explore some important themes that crop up in a lot of Shakespeare's more serious plays.

In fact, this play comes very close to being a tragedy. Parts of the plot are quite similar to the plot of Shakespeare's great tragedy *Romeo and Juliet.* Here, Hero pretends to die in order to deceive others (in this case her lover Claudio).

At many times in the play, betrayal, hatred and grief seem to be only just below the surface.

What are the main themes in the play?

Love – The play shows us that love can take many forms. Young love can be passionate, but it is fragile and can be easily broken or lost (as happens between Claudio and Hero).

The love between Benedick and Beatrice is different. For them, it's almost as if love and hate are very closely related. Love seems to turn to hate (and back again) very easily – much to the amusement of the audience!

Other kinds of love feature in the play as well. There is the love of a father for his daughter, for example, as well as the kind of love that you can find between close friends.

In the end, though, it is love, not hate, that wins through. After all, there's nothing quite like a happy ending!

Deception – *Much Ado About Nothing* is full of trickery and deceit. Some deceptions in the play are intended to cause harm. Claudio and Don Pedro are tricked into believing that Hero has been unfaithful, which results in Claudio refusing to marry her. Notice that Hero responds to that deception with another: she tricks Claudio and Don Pedro into thinking that she is dead.

Other deceptions are more playful. Benedick and Beatrice are tricked into believing that they love each other, and as a result they do actually fall in love.

There are also many other smaller deceptions in the play. Don Pedro agrees to pretend to be Claudio when he dances with Hero, but the audience is not sure whether Don Pedro can be trusted. Will he deceive Claudio and try to woo Hero himself?

At the ball, Claudio also pretends to be Benedick (when talking to Don Pedro), just as Don Pedro pretends that he doesn't know that he is talking to Claudio. At the same ball, Benedick and Beatrice find themselves dancing together, each not knowing who they are dancing with.

Honour – The highpoint of the play is at the church, when Claudio refuses to marry Hero because he believes that she has been unfaithful to him.

In Shakespeare's time, honour was very important. A woman's honour depended on her being a virgin when she married, and sexual relations before marriage would be catastrophic for her. Marriage would be impossible and life in a nunnery might be the best that could happen.

A woman's infidelity would also reflect very badly on her family. This is why Leonato is so upset by the accusation against Hero: it is a shame from which he cannot recover either.

Shakespeare's words

The language in *Much Ado About Nothing* is very rich. Sometimes Shakespeare wants to make us laugh; at other times he wants us to know how characters feel.

The dialogue between Benedick and Beatrice is rich in humour. For example, Beatrice says that Benedick will hang on his new friend Claudio *'like a disease'*. She could have made lots of different comparisons, but comparing him to is disease is startling and funny – as well as showing how she seems to feel about him. This is a good example of Shakespeare using a **simile** (a comparison using 'as', 'like' or 'than').

Shakespeare also uses language to make fun of Dogberry, who tries to speak using important words, but ends up tying himself in knots. A good example is when he is describing Borachio and Conrade's offences to Don Pedro and Claudio (see page 45): *'Moreover ... secondarily ... sixth and lastly ... thirdly ... and, to conclude ...'*

Shakespeare also uses language to sharpen our understanding of how various characters feel. When Claudio refuses to marry Hero at the church, he says to Leonato, *'Give not this rotten orange to your friend.'* The audience in Shakespeare's time would have been very familiar with buying fruit that looked fine on the outside, but was rotten on the inside. Describing Hero as a rotten orange is a way of saying that, although she looks fine on the outside, she is in fact *'rotten'* on the inside, having been unfaithful to him.